James] [Hall

Block Island

James] [Hall

Block Island

ISBN/EAN: 9783337373948

Printed in Europe, USA, Canada, Australia, Japan

Cover: Foto ©Andreas Hilbeck / pixelio.de

More available books at **www.hansebooks.com**

BLOCK ISLAND:

A HAND-BOOK, WITH MAP,

FOR THE GUIDANCE OF SUMMER VISITORS, TELLING HOW
TO REACH THAT PLEASANT LITTLE PLACE OF
RESORT, AND WHAT TO DO ON
GETTING THERE:

TOGETHER WITH

DESCRIPTION AND
SENTIMENT CALCULATED TO ADORN
AN OTHERWISE PLAIN TALE, AND TO
EXCITE THE INTEREST OF THE APATHETIC, YET
WITHOUT TOO WIDELY DEPARTING FROM THE STRICT TRUTH.

By "BEN MUSH,"
Staff Correspondent of the Norwich Morning Bulletin.

"And the pale health-seeker findeth there
The wine of life in its pleasant air."—*Whittier*.

JAMES HALL: NORWICH, C
1877.

Printed by THE BULLETIN COMPANY, Norwich, Conn.

Block Island: A Hand-Book.

HERE are but few physiques with enough elasticity to endure, without some slight interruption at times, the exhaustion of America's high-pressure social and business life, augmented as it is almost every year by the intensity of the summer's heat; and even of those who are not particularly burdened with tasks and cares, there are but few to whom an occasional change of thought and surroundings does not afford both temporary gratification and more or less permanent and varied good. And so, overcome with ennui or the weather, or both, over-taxed in mind or body or depressed in spirits, all classes of humanity rush eagerly every summer to the woods, the mountains or the sea, for a longer or shorter stay, seeking that physical, mental or spiritual refreshment which the old routine, and "nature's sweet restorer" do not give at home.

The industrious artizan, with or without his family, or perhaps with gayly bedecked sweetheart, goes off for a day's sail and an old-fashioned shore dinner. The school mistress, worn out with her poorly paid labor and the innumerable vexations of a year, seeks, for a week or two, some quiet spot, where, amid the glories of nature and quite translated from her wonted environment, her cramped up soul can expand, her sweeter fancies, pent like the possibilities of a hyacinth bulb in winter, revive and blossom, and her material system derive a fresh stock of much needed vigor. The thriving tradesman, who wants his wife and daughters to take just as much comfort out of life, put on just as much style, and see just as much of the world, its beauties, celebrities and wonders as his next door neighbor's, or a little more, benevolently packs his family off to some favorite resort, and then goes after them himself.

The languid invalid, either morbidly making a martyr of herself by concealing from solicitous friends her real condition or exaggerated fears, or else making martyrs of them by her moods and whims, is sent to try the virtue of a new society and climate. Parents with children who poorly bear the rigors of summer in the city, hasten to find more salubrious surroundings for the sickly little ones. Some thoroughly heart-sick wife or mother, perhaps, whose bitter grief and state of mind is concealed from the world by a singularly sweet face and sympathetic manner, desperately seeks the utmost possible isolation from painful associations, and thus unconsciously regains her wonted peace and equilibrium, if not her former joy.

Merchants and brokers, whose affairs have been complicated

and unprosperous; lawyers and bankers, who have the custody of a score of burdensome trusts, beside their own personal business affairs; overwrought professional men, ministers to men's bodily and mental cravings or ailments, moulders of public' opinion, statesmen, officers of the government, lay aside their several duties like an oppressive garment; and in fresh and hardy sports, in quiet communion with lovely and ever-teaching nature, or in delightful intercourse with chance acquaintances of experience and taste, gain new life and strength, new ideas of beauty, new philosophy, new memories, new purposes, and new inspirations to their several and manifold tasks. And not only men, but also women—women of large hearts and tender sympathies, of minds and of means, of high aims and social position, to whose modest but infinite influence the world is indebted for far more than half of its true happiness, if not of its moral progress.

Then, too, there are the butterflies of fashion who seek to know what flowers of idle pleasure, folly and excitement bloom without the too familiar pale of local society; the folks who find the city lonely when every one else has gone; the designing mothers of marriageable daughters; the designing daughters whose mothers let them go alone; the impecunious and designing but otherwise eligible young man; and even more artful adventurers of both sexes, who thrive upon the weaknesses of mankind, and go to places of rendezvous for their prey.

And so the catalogue might be spun out indefinitely: for the eight great classes of people who possess one or two, or all, or

none of the three chief agencies in the world—money, brains
and principle—are sub-divided infinitessimally; and every one
of these innumerable species of humanity has some occasion
for patronizing the summer resort.

WHY GO TO BLOCK ISLAND?

But no spot under heaven, however charming, is equally
well adapted to the diversified tastes of all these classes; and
no one will wisely seek any resort, however popular, without
first having a tolerably fair idea how it differs from others, and
how well suited it is to his or her peculiar needs. Hence this
little sketch of Block Island's characteristics.

In the first place, no "distinguished personages" habitually
visit it. Gen. Grant was known to do so on one occasion; but
he only stayed a part of a day, and was so mortally sea-sick
thereafter that he never again ventured within a hundred
miles of the spot. No famous actresses nor merchant princes
nor men of letters have here their tasteful villas. The closest
approaches to a cottage on the island are a government life
saving station as regards architecture, and a country farm-
house in point of domestic economy. No landscape gardener
has here plied his art, there being neither flower bed nor forest,
shrub or grateful grove to be seen, even solitary shade or fruit
trees being rare.

There is no racing here. The Block Island horse that can
go more than five miles an hour yet remains to be discovered,

while few of them can more than keep up with an ox-team. Besides, the vehicles and roads are not especially conducive to quick transit. The only competition in speed to be witnessed hereabouts is between the numerous sailing craft that circumnavigate the island. Nor is there danger of youthful morals being debauched by either gambling or drink. A peaceful game of billiards, an evening of whist or euchre, and languid attempts at mumble-t'-peg, are the extremes of the former; while of the latter, even so moderate an indulgence as a soothing claret punch is only possible when one has brought his own Bordeaux, and is willing to sacrifice his own sweet idleness so far as to concoct the beverage himself.

The only balls, properly so-called, yet witnessed on the island, have been of codfish and twine; though more than one unostentatious, but thoroughly delightful dance, has been had with piano music at some of the hotels. These establishments, by the way, do not quite equal the Windsor or Grand Union in stupendous grandeur, appointments, fare or service. Flies have been found in the cream jug, and one often sits five minutes at the table without being able to secure attendance. But I shall have more to say of the hotels directly.

Generally speaking, one may say that contact with modern civilization has, as yet, but faintly tarnished the prevalent primitiveness of the honest, staid old islanders, whose life is spent in sea-fishing and farming; who cure their cod in oderiferous huts, and gather for manure the sea-weed which is strewn by the tides upon the beach; who ride and draw their produce

in ox-carts, along dusty, stone-walled roads, grind their corn
in antiquated windmills, and stack their hay under a sheltering
hillside; from whom every wayfarer, stranger or friend, wins a
salute, and to whom jails and constables are as useless as gar-
ters are to whales.   Indeed, such slightly impaired, unadorned
simplicity and robustness of character is, in the present day,
well worth going far to see.

Besides this quaintness of scene and manner, and notwith-
standing the apparent drawbacks at which I have hinted, the
island has many substantial charms.

The mild sea air is a most wonderful tonic; and as the ocean
surrounds the spot on all sides, this peculiar advantage is en-
joyed to the utmost.   The luxurious and invigorating salt water
bath can be had here under favorable circumstances, the beach
being one of the finest on the Atlantic coast, and having an
advantage over almost all others in being better sheltered, and
being washed by warmer water.   The temperature of the air
is always lower than upon the main land, usually ranging between 70° and 80° in the shade through midsummer, and almost never touching 90°.   Moreover, some peculiar quality—
the moisture, perhaps—of this sea air really makes the same
degree of heat appreciably more tolerable than on the main
land; and in addition to this, there is an almost constant breeze
playing through the verandas and shutters, night and day.
Mosquitoes are not altogether unknown; and yet they are never seen except in unusually dry seasons, and then only in small
numbers.

There is a much wider range of prices of board here than at most other resorts, the public houses varying in size and convenience from the large, well appointed sea-side hotel to the modest farm-house; and the latter are so nicely managed that if one has simple tastes and but limited means, and knows, in advance, what to expect, he will be very well suited with the accommodations; while on the other hand, at the more pretentious houses, most of the luxuries and refinements which a fastidious taste demands and wealth can alone supply, are attainable with comparatively little difficulty. Custom allows a very wide latitude to choice in the matter of toilets, many ladies bringing to the island but a single dress beside their cambric wrappers, and boots and hats that have grown too shabby for city wear; gentlemen wearing all day their own cast-off winter clothing. At the same time, there are suitable opportunities for the display of diamonds, silks and lace, if one has a mind to expose such a wardrobe to the ravages of the moist sea air. Formality can be indulged in to almost any extent, but is not in the least obligatory. One can make as much of a hermit of himself as he likes; yet most excellent society is to be found, Philadelphia, Chicago, Buffalo, Troy, New York, and Boston, and many nearer centres of culture contributing largely to the floating population of the island; so that no one of true refinement and education can fail to find congenial company.

He, too, who loves to commune with nature, as well as with his fellow man, and seeks the refreshment and renovation of his soul as well as of his body, has here the restless, changeable, now soothingly quiet, now magnificently tumultuous sea, gorgeous sunsets and wide spreading views, gently undulating meadows, and some grand and picturesque cliffs.

To sum up briefly, then, I should say that Block Island is a resort unusually free from the objectionable features of a fast American life possessing happily combined facilities for charming, but subdued social intercourse and sweet retirement, a rarely salubrious climate, an excellent beach, and simple yet varied and inspiring scenery : as well adapted to those in humble circumstances in life as to the more prosperous, and admirably calculated to restore the sick in body and in soul. Indeed, the spirit of the place is admirably embodied in that poem of Whittier, "The wreck of the Palatine," which no one should fail to read who thinks of going there.

ITS HISTORY AND TOPOGRAPHY.

Before proceeding from the general to the particular features of the island, and offering a few practical suggestions to the visitor, it is perhaps worth while to very briefly hint at the history of the place, and to hastily sketch its physical outlines. The history of Block Island, however, has been treated more comprehensively than would be consistent with either the character or limits of this work, by the Rev. S. T. Livermore, whose book will be given to the public this season, and may be relied on as both interesting and accurate. There are other excellent works of the kind also extant. Suffice it therefore to

say here, that John Verrazzano, a Florentine explorer touched
this island in 1524; and Adrian Blok, a Dutch navigator, after
whom the island was named, in 1614. Neither of them, however, established any settlement. English colonists from Connecticut and Rhode Island had some trifling communication
with the natives, who were Narragansett Indians, and whose
name for the island was Manisees. In 1635 one John Oldham
having ventured over from Saybrook with too little protection,
was murdered by the savages, upon whom revenge was subse-
quently wrought by an armed force despatched by Gov. En-
dicott, of Massachusetts. By a grant from the civil authority
of that colony, and by purchase from the natives, a title was
acquired to Block Island in 1661; and a reservation being
made for the maintenance of the gospel, the remainder of the
land was equally divided, and the first permanent settlement
established. In 1664 the residents were notified that the col-
onial government of Rhode Island regarded the plantation as
within its jurisdiction; and in 1672 the town adopted the
name of New Shoreham, its present post-office address. Upon
this quiet beginning over two centuries of almost uneventful
history and almost complete isolation from the main land have
ensued, the French and English wars of the eighteenth century leading to some not very violent contests for possession,
and the residents being subjected to quite trifling depredation.
Her location prevented her people from taking any active
share in the revolution, or in the war of 1812-14; but in the
late civil war she sent volunteers to both the army and navy.

LOCATION.

Long Island terminates at the east, in two long prongs; one, with a chain of islands reaching nearly to Watch Hill, Rhode Island, constituting an imperfect barrier across the sound; and the other, part of a coast line which doubtless in some prehistoric period reached out to Cuttyhunk, or Martha's Vineyard, but now is marked only by the solitary islet which bears the name of its Dutch discoverer. Block Island is about 16 miles east north-east of Montauk Point, and 14 south south-west of Point Judith; and is distant, approximately, 25 miles from Newport, 50 from Providence, 32 from Stonington, 45 from New London, and 60 from Norwich.

HOW TO GET THERE.

One of the best facilities for reaching Block Island is the steamer of the Norwich and New London Steamboat Company, advertised in the appendix of this work. Last year the company ran the Ella on this route, but this season will probably put on a new and swifter boat. The old one was staunch and comfortable, and managed by gentlemanly, cautious and skillful officers; and the new one certainly will be, too. Until outside of Fisher's Island, off Stonington, the steamer on this line never experiences rough water; and from that point over to the island, even in bad weather (which is rare in the summer season) the trip is short. This boat will run Mondays, Wednesdays, and Fridays. On the alternate week days the

Canonicus makes a like trip from Providence, touching at Newport. She, too, is a well appointed, well officered and safe conveyance. Besides these steamers, there was last year a sailing vessel from Newport to the island, carrying the mails, but undesirable for passengers. This may be replaced by a faster boat this season, making daily trips, but the details of the plan are not known at this writing.

No New Englander need be told how to reach Providence, nor much about its hotels. If he be entirely ignorant on the latter point, let him consult the advertising appendix of this book. A simple inquiry on arrival will enable him to find the wharf of the Canonicus, which is not more than quarter of a mile from the railway station.

Norwich is readily accessible from the north, east and west by rail. The New York and New England Railroad, which has become a favorite trunk route from Boston to New York and the west, leases the Norwich and Worcester road, and brings passengers to this city and to New London, at which latter place they may take the magnificent sound steamers of the so-called Norwich Line. The New London Northern Division of the Vermont Central, which makes close connections with the Boston and Albany road at Palmer, and with the Hartford, Providence and Fishkill road at Willimantic, also passes through Norwich, its trains usually stopping at a different station from those on the Norwich and Worcester road. Neither, however, is more than half a mile from the dock of the Block Island steamer. As the sail down the Thames, at

the head of which Norwich is situated, is particularly lovely in
the summer time, many will prefer to take the boat at this
point, if equally convenient in other respects, to doing so at
New London or Stonington.

New London, however, is perhaps preferable by those coming by way of New York, whether they take the spacious and
luxurious steamers on the sound, or a through Pullman
coach over the safe, smooth road of the Shore Line route.   Passengers wanting a good night's rest or a well served meal in
New London, can find both at the Crocker house, not far from
either railway station or landing.

LOCAL TOPOGRAPHY.

As will be seen, from the map in the front of this little volume,
Block Island, in shape, somewhat resembles a pear, stem end up.
It is about seven miles in length, and from three to four broad
in the widest part.   At the northern and south-eastern extremities are light-houses.   Its surface is a constant series of slight
undulations, a large number of small ponds nestling here and
there among the hillocks.   Just north of the middle of the
island is an immense pond which communicates with the ocean
to the westward, and is therefore salt, and which so nearly di-
vides the upper and lower parts of the island that one ap-
proaching it from the north-westward thinks there are two instead of one.   The next larger of these little areas of water is
near the northern extremity.   Bold cliffs, from one hundred to

two hundred feet high, overlook much of the coast—the highest being on the eastern side of the upper part of the island, at the place called Clay Head, and about the south-western, southern, and south-eastern shores. There are, also, quite prominent cliffs just to the south of the government breakwater. The harbor is on the eastern side, on the southern skirt of a deep concavity of the coast line; and in this immediate vicinity are gathered most of the hotels, small country stores and residences, the post-office, and huts in which the fish are cured— all too few and too scattered to constitute a village, yet the nearest semblance of one on the island. About a mile and-a-half in the interior are one of the churches, the town house, and a half-a-dozen other stores and residences. The homes of the farmers and fishermen are thinly scattered over the rest of the surface.

Of the map prefaced to these pages it may be observed, by the way, that it makes no pretensions to scientific accuracy, but is simply a sketch. The hills are not indicated, nor the location of all the houses. It will be found, however, to answer all the practical purposes of a guide to summer visitors.

FIRST IMPRESSIONS OF THE ISLAND UNFAVORABLE.

In this connection, a word of warning may not be out of place. The landing is not an attractive looking neighborhood; and what with its appearance, the odor emanating from the fish curing houses, the warmth and the dusty roads, one's first impression of the place, especially if he have only come over for the two or three hours that the steamer stops, is often unfavorable to the island, and he goes away with a deep-seated, but unjust prejudice. Indeed, the visitor who has come for a fortnight's stay, is sometimes disappointed for a few hours. But Block Island, like some of our best friends, shows its worst side to us first, and a little charitable patience and familiarity soon reveal to an appreciative person, its many modest but truly winsome and poetic charms.

THE HOTELS.

Of the hotels it is necessary to say but little here. As we have remarked in the introductory pages of this work, one can find anything in the range from a summer hotel with modern appointments and prices to little establishments that differ from neat old farm houses more in name than in fare or service. In the appendix to this volume, which should be carefully perused, can be found the names of most of these caravanseries; and their several locations are indicated on the map. As one approaches the island, he always sees the national flag floating from the tops of the hotels, and on landing finds their vans and carriages awaiting him at the wharf. Most of them have been greatly enlarged and improved since last season.

BATHING.

One of the first privileges of his life on Block Island to which the visitor's thoughts will turn, will be the bathing.

Unless he be remarkably robust, however, he will be unwise to indulge himself for two or three days. Although one scarcely realizes it, there is such a decided change in the character of the atmosphere that at first this alone will afford as much of a tonic as is wholesome for most people. Moreover, it is unwise to bathe more frequently than every other day to begin with, nor to stay in more than five or ten minutes at a time. It is no uncommon thing for people in their eagerness and enthusiasm to overdo in this respect, and to suffer in consequence. Riding or walking to the beach, sitting upon an outspread blanket shawl or the camp-stool one has been prudent enough to bring, watching the youngsters at their sports on the wet sand, and studying the now sportive, now awkward bathers, and their ludicrous appearance on emerging from the surf, are usually enough to satisfy most people for a few days.

Nearly all of the shores of the island are stony or gravelly. Almost the only good stretch of clean sand is to be found along the bay to the north of the harbor, half-a-mile or more from the landing. Here is to be found a nice shelving beach and an ocean bottom free from pit-holes, stones or weeds; and here are arrayed the rude huts in which the bathers robe and disrobe. These houses, owned by the respective proprietors of the hotels, are, in the winter time, hauled up on the high bank back of the beach to keep them out of reach of the heavy seas of winter—being restored to their proper places as soon as required by summer visitors. Thus far they have been only too few, and an agitation for an increased number will

2

probably be necessary this season. Conveyance to the beach is furnished, to those who do not like the rather toilsome walk over a soft sandy road, by the hotel proprietors, who run teams, for the convenience of the bathers. The use of the bathing houses is given gratuitously by the proprietors to their own guests; but special rates for conveyance have to be agreed upon at the opening of the season. They differ somewhat at the various houses. Most people prefer to bring their own bathing suits with them, including oil skin caps and sandals; but suits, of the only two simple garments really requisite, are procurable on the island.

The best time for bathing is when the tide is out, or has just turned to come in, for two reasons: first, when the tide is full, or running out, there is a slight undertow never felt at any other time; and second, the slope of the bottom, just within the water's edge, is more gradual at low than high tide, one being able to go out seventy-five or one hundred feet from the shore at the former. For the benefit of those who take this into consideration, a tide table is given in the back part of this work.

A rather more important consideration to the visitor is the relation of his bathing hour to meal time. It is better to bathe on an empty stomach than a full one; hence it is customary to go to the beach about ten or eleven A. M., irrespective of tide, getting back in time to improve on the bath-house toilet, and get a half hour's doze before dinner. When there is a high tide in the morning, some prefer to take their baths at four or five o'clock in the afternoon. If there be ample conveyance and bath-house accommodations, however, it is much pleasanter for all to go in about the same time, because it gives more confidence to the timid, more company to the courageous, and more fun to those who go merely as spectators.

BOATING.

One of the pleasantest episodes of Block Island life is the occasional sail. Everyone, ladies included, will want to indulge in at least one, and many in more. One of the most common trips is around the island, on a fair day; or one may go a fishing, of which more anon; or one may take a short moon-light sail; or again on a moonless night, go out to witness that strange and beautiful phenomenon, the marine phosphorescence. One may, perhaps, catch a little rougher sea on these occasions than he anticipated, and suffer a bit from seasickness; or may reach the same end by the different agency of the lazy, deceitful swell of a calm. A lady may, from a failure to heed the skipper's warning, lose a hat or a veil; or a coat or a dress may be sprinkled or soiled; a mist may thicken into fog; or some other trifling contretemps may be experienced; but one can rely implicitly on being safe, and all these incidents have their amusing phases. Even were they not enjoyable in themselves, they would be vastly more than compensated for by the novelty or excitement of the adventure. Then there are new glimpses to be had of the island, the sight of Mother

Carey's chickens toward which the true sailor manifests such a peculiar tenderness, the sportive porpoise and the occasionally visible whale; the skipper's quaint expressions and good-natured chat, his slight peculiarities of pronunciation, his nautical technicalities, his quiet humor and cleverness, and his simple anecdotes and old-fashioned traditions, particularly if one can get him telling some story of a wreck : all of which combine with the dextrous handling of helm and sail, the dash and sparkle of the foaming, lapping waves, the fresh breeze, and the possible competition with another craft making the same trip, to take one completely outside of his wonted sphere of thought, and entertain him immensely. Such chances for seeing new phases of human character and nature's wondrous works are too few, even in a lifetime.

One has little difficulty in finding boats for these excursions. Both the old sailors who have cleaned up or made over their working boats for the use of pleasure parties, and their younger, more enterprising sons who have ventured their hard won gains in more pretentious and elegant craft, are so eager for custom that they are ever cruising about in search of the eager landsman, waylaying him—though not too intrusively—upon the the road, or addressing him upon the veranda of his hotel. Their terms are generally very moderate, though they know how to drive a good bargain ; and their boats, though quite different in model and size, are seaworthy and safe ; so that one needs bother about little beyond the condition of his purse, the size and tastes of his party, and the quality of his lunch, if such concomitant to the expedition be deemed desirable.

FISHING.

Scarcely a summer visitor comes to the island who does not want to know something about the fishing; and certainly after, if not before, his first sail with the native navigators, his eagerness for this variety of sport will have reached a high pitch. The diversion is one in which only the sterner sex will care to indulge; and, after the first experience, only the sterner of the stern, unless, perhaps, they have the patience to angle for flounders or cunners off the end of the breakwater, or are content with the mild excitement of catching perch or black bass in one of the inland ponds. Yet there is rare sport to be had, in ordinary seasons, out upon the briny deep; and the man who has visited Block Island, and caught neither a cod nor a bluefish, has missed one of the most glorious opportunities which the place affords for recreation. I mention cod and blue-fish particularly, because one is more likely to find these; but the mackerel, which run in such shoals that when they are to be had at all, they can be seined; the rarer and choicer bonita, the aldermanic swordfish, the sea bass, and other denizens of the deep, are also to be caught on occasions, and afford equally exhilarating sport.

The principal catch of codfish by those to whom its capture is a means of livelihood is made in the spring and fall. But during the summer, on a decent day, one can almost always find them on a bank some six miles to the south-eastward of the harbor, at a depth of from a hundred to a hundred and fifty feet. Ten and twelve pounders are the average, with now and then an approach to twenty or thirty; while the man who takes a forty pound cod, in the summer time, is a hero for a month. Cod fishing is nominally still fishing, the boats heaving to on the bank, and every half hour or so, beating up against the wind to offset the drifting. The bait is a bit of some worthless variety of fish, which, with the tackle, are provided by the boatman. The precautions which the amateur needs to take are to insist on having the hooks sharpened, the bait fresh, ice in the hold to preserve the catch, and fresh water in the boat's earthenware jug. But more than these, it is important that one is sure his skipper knows just exactly where to find the fish, especially if there happen to be a fog and he has to sail by the compass and guess, instead of by his bearings from landmarks.

The blue-fish is much smaller than the cod, but is far more gamey. The cod resists but languidly; the blue-fish is as demonstrative as the pickerel. Blue-fish are taken with almost any kind of bait, a bit of rag being the veteran fisherman's chief reliance, and trolling a few hundred rods off shore. Their pursuit is more of a lottery than that of the cod; but the excitement when one wins the prize of a successful day, amply repays the risk.

Indeed, even though one has poor luck as regards the gross aggregate of captures, the novelty of the experience, the ludicrous appearance of one's sea-sick companions, the reaction of magnificent appetite and tingling vigor one enjoys next day if he has been thoroughly sea-sick himself, the consciousness of dining off your own fish chowder, the skipper's philosophy and humor, the sunburn, the skin sawn fingers, the rivalry with other parties out the same day, the half-concealed curiosity of the sailor on the dock who wanders up to inventory your spoils as you come in, and the indescribable but inspiriting romance of the adventure make the day a pleasant one for the time being, and still pleasanter to look back upon.

Usually the amateur carries off his biggest fish to his hotel or boarding-house for his next day's dinner and as a trophy; the remainder, by the unwritten, but generally recognized law of custom, are the skipper's perquisites, as are also any half-consumed papers of tobacco, or modicum of spirits, one may thoughtlessly leave in some odd corner of the old craft.

APPROPRIATE READING.

It is the experience of many that one never has so little leisure as when he has nothing to do. It is astonishing how little reading or writing or fancy work one can accomplish during a summer's idling. At Block Island, people spend so much time in preparing for or dressing after the bath, on trips hither and thither on the water or ashore, in visiting with fellow idlers upon the broad veranda, in twilight reveries, in music or dancing, or in the more intellectual yet social whist, with

possible liquid accompaniments, that they have little time for
reading; and often carry their books home almost unopened.
Yet I would advise everyone, who comes for more than a
week's stay, to bring a book or two, but to be particular what
he brings.   Leave novels behind, unless you have one you especially want to read.   Leave philosophy and every thing in the
way of study.   Take nothing but poetry, and that choose with
care.   The freedom from absorbing physical and mental occupation which one enjoys here is especially favorable to the ex-
pansion of the esthetic instincts ; and one soon finds his poetic
nature quickened to a susceptibility almost unknown amid the
pressing cares and occupations of ordinary life.   I don't mean
that he feels like writing verses.   He is too languid for that.
He is in the passive, not the active mood.   But he is peculiarly
alive to beautiful, grand and inspiring ideas ; and so, if provided
with just the right means, he finds himself at a happy stage of
soul culture.   Such means are to be found in the glorious sunsets, ever varying cloud forms, the soft air and hues of twilight,
the calm moonlit nights, the reverie on the beach, the solitary
ramble, the innumerable and almost monotonous undulations of
the wide fields, the bold, lonely cliffs, in the vast infinity
of the ocean, the immensity of the heavenly vault, and the for-
tissimo and pianissimo of the waves' symphony ; and the sensi-
bility thereto and to moral beauty and grandeur is excited not
a little by an occasional bit of sentiment from the great word-
artists.   .

Jean Ingelow's poetry is, perhaps, in feeling and description, most in harmony with the spirit of the island, its waves and sea-weed, its wastes of sand, and scanty growth of bent. But Wordsworth and Tennyson will also be read here with a deeper tenderness and meaning, and Whittier's "Tent on the Beach," and the "Wreck of the Palatine." So, too, with Byron's "Childe Harold," and indeed with all poetry which deals with nature rather than character and story. This, of course, includes "The Beauties of Ruskin," which contain suggestions regarding nature which one will find especially acceptable here, and can apply and assimilate more readily than under any other circumstances. By all means, then, take a little—and only a little—poetry with you to Block Island.

THE DRIVES.

Driving will, for some time to come, be indulged in on Block Island as a means, rather than an end. Nothing luxurious in the way of a vehicle is to be had, the best being an old fashioned buggy, or a weak springed democrat wagon, unless perchance, one has been able to bring over her own little phaeton from the main land. Moreover, the roads are either hilly and rather stony, (although the town authorities have vastly improved them of late years) or else over soft sand, which if anything is more wearisome than the stones. Then, too, a horse there which can go faster than a four-mile-an-hour walk is phenomenal. Yet there are several points of interest well worth visiting, of which detailed mention is made elsewhere;

and with such objects in view, the little drawbacks here suggested sink into a nameless insignificance. Besides, if one sets out expecting absolutely nothing in the way of roadside charms, but keeps alert to what little beauty there may happen to lie about his path, he will be pleasantly rather than otherwise disappointed.

The waysides yield a rather scanty turf, and the grass is allowed to grow tall and gather dust; but the dew and occasional showers keep it tolerably fresh. The daisy, though somewhat stunted, and the thistle are quite abundant, and also white clover and the blackberry sprays, the last named penetrating or clambering over the homely, yet picturesque, grey and lichen covered stone walls which every where take the place of fences. The wild brier rose, the humble sorrel with its occasional crimson leaf, the wild jessamine and strumonium also enliven the way.

Another flower which grows in great abundance on the island is the water lily, to be found in several of the many little pools nestling among the innumerable hillocks. The rambler, however, must from the first abandon all thought of gathering these lovely and fragrant blossoms himself. They are as tempting and near yet as inaccessible as the food and drink of Tantalus. One must, therefore, be content either to enjoy the sight of them from afar, or gain possession only through the barefooted urchins who carry bunches of them around in their hands for sale.

To those who drive on the island, one practical suggestion is

necessary. Many of the roads are private ways, and are cross-
ed by gates. The islanders are exceedingly obliging in grant-
ing their use to visitors ; but, very naturally, they like these
gates kept closed. Certainly the trouble of shutting them after
going through is a very trifling condition to the privilege. In
one or two instances, juvenile porters volunteer their services,
and feel amply compensated by the toss of a nickle.

RAMBLES ON THE BEACH.

Some of the disadvantages attendant upon driving here
equally beset the pedestrian's rambles. The roads are sandy,
dusty or rugged, and there is scarcely enough in the wayside
attractions to make a stroll desirable for itself alone. Good
vigorous walkers, however, often prefer to visit some of the
points of interest afoot rather than ride, taking tramps of six
and eight and even ten miles at a time. Yet very few, especially
among the ladies, care to undertake any thing of this sort.

However, to those who love solitude and reverie, and have a
taste for the curious, there are many charms about a clamber
down the cliffs near the Ocean View hotel, and a stroll thence,
or up near the bathing beach, along the water's edge. In either
case one certainly ought to carry an old woolen shawl over his
arm, and, if so disposed, may take a book of poems along too.
Such rambles are enjoyable, both when there is a heavy surf tumb-
ling in, thundering and breaking into spray over the great wet
boulders, and when the beach is only lapped with playful rip-

ples and the tide is out.   At the latter time one finds dainty bits
of sea-weed, pretty little pebbles and shells, jelly-fish and star-
fish, and queer looking crabs; none of them especially wondrous or beautiful, and yet quite attractive; and one's hands are
soon so full that, child-like, he has to throw away half his treas-
ures in order to hold the rest.   By and by one gets a little
weary, and then spreads his shawl upon the sand, sits him
down, and communes either with the poet or with the waves,
their majesty or music soothing the spirit into reverence and
reverie, and stirring sweet thoughts in the soul.

THE SPRINGS.

A less sentimental, but possibly more popular stroll is at evening, down to the springs which give the Spring house its
name, and whose location is indicated on the map.   They are
two in number; one a clear, sweet water, and the other strongly tinctured with iron.   Both are curbed and provided with
cups; and a convenient platform, with seats, is at hand, where-
on one may rest, flirt with his companion, and study the cloud
forms or dying twilight tints, while recovering breath for his
return.

BEACON HILL.

One of the first places to which one should go is Beacon
Hill, near the centre of the island and at its highest elevation.
It is situated about half-a-mile west of the church, on the right

hand side of the only road running clear across the island, and is
easily found without more specific direction than to look at
your map, and be sure to take the right road past the church.
We believe there is a carriage road leading to its top; but most
persons, having ridden out thus far from the landing, will prefer hitching their team to a fence post, and clambering up the turf-
covered slope afoot. The best time to go is immediately after
supper, in order to see the sunset; or a party may find it
pleasant to start earlier, and bring their suppers in a basket.

The great attraction of Beacon Hill is the magnificent view it
affords on a clear day.

Without actually being very high up, one here looks down,
almost as a bird in air, upon the undulating surface of the
island, the languid but constant heaving of whose broad bosom
is suggestive of a usually calm soul, mildly agitated with pleasure.
The winding roads, the network of stone fences, the brown and
treeless meadows with here and there a dark green field of
waving corn, a haystack or a picturesque windmill, the various
sized ponds, the almost solitary farm-house, the church and the
clump of hotels and dwellings over near the harbor, alone constitute a landscape restful and charming to the eye. And then
all around this picture, except where the bluff at the southeast
corner of the island breaks the circle, the ocean stretches, the
infinity of its expanse forming a soothing yet inspiring contrast
to the narrow and tortuous streets of cities, and the hampering
limitations of circumstance and toil. Then, too, its never
quiet waters, like the infinite intellect cresting into countless even

though transitory thoughts, richly reward a lingering contem-
plation.   One looks to the south and east and tries to estimate
the thousands of miles that intervene between this and other
shores; and then turns with a mild curiosity to identify Point
Judith and Watch Hill, the extremity of Montauk, the low-
lying Gardiner's Island, and the faint line of the Connecticut
coast beyond which one discerns the setting sun, which, unless
one revives a few principles of his spherical trigonometry will
seem a great deal farther north than it ought to be.   At last
one's gaze is lifted to the clouds, which he is almost sure to
find away to the north and west, hovering over the main land,
if nowhere else.   Even though he may not have looked at his
Ruskin recently, and been helped thereby to a keener appreci-
ation of hue and form, he will here find a variety and richness
of color and majesty of sculpture that seem too limitless to be
wholly grasped, and will feel again the enlargement of spirit
which becomes so frequent and profitable an experience amid
this island scenery.

THE SOUTH CLIFFS AND LIGHT-HOUSE.

A better known and to some a more attractive quarter of the
island is the neighborhood of the cliffs at the south-eastern corner, where stands the new light-house.   If one has heard them
previously described, and then makes a circuit of the island in
a sailboat, he is disappointed in their appearance, regards them
as uninteresting, and even doubts the statement that they are

nearly two hundred feet above the water's edge. As pleasure or pain is the greater for coming contrary to anticipation, it may be well for the visitor to postpone his trip to these cliffs by land until after he has circumvented the island by water. He will find the main route, when he does undertake it, sufficiently indicated on the map; only that he must expect to pass through three or four gates on the private road which forms the continuation of the highway, and follow an unfenced but clearly defined path the last half of the journey; or the strong and adventurous pedestrian may, at low tide, follow the coast line down from the breakwater, occasionally clambering over a boulder, or scrambling up on the bluff to escape some particularly large wave. The distance, in a bee line, from the harbor is not over two miles and-a-half, but is a walk or drive of four.

To a great many persons the light-house will be an object of much interest. It belongs to the highest of the several classes into which the human sign-posts along the highway of nations are divided; the structure costing no less than $75,000, and its blaze being visible nearly thirty miles at sea. The keeper, who, with his assistant, lives on the premises, is a courteous and obliging official, and is equally attentive whether his kindness be acknowledged with verbal or more substantial gratuities. The ascent of the long spiral iron staircase, even by ladies and invalids, is amply repaid by a sight of the immense and singularly arranged apparatus, and by the interesting information to be elicited concerning it. And then, when one has satisfied his curiosity regarding the light, he should ask to see the steam fog-horn in the low wooden building adjacent, even though he may not hear its powerful melancholy intermittent blast until some other day, from his hotel up near the harbor. If, however, one is particularly eager to see and hear this singular piece of mechanism in operation, he can do so any Monday forenoon, at which time, for purposes of test and discipline, it is always used for an hour or more.

The cliffs are worth, at least, two visits. The first should be paid on a comparatively calm day, the expedition setting out, say, at four or five o'clock, with a good lunch basket in the wagon, which might be reinforced with a pail of milk from some farm-house along the road. After one has "done" the light-house, rambled an hour on the beach at the bottom of the cliffs, and clambered up to their crest again, he will be impatient to have the shawls spread and the baskets opened. Then, while he discusses the contents, the grandeur of the ocean view, and the varying depth and softness of color of water and sky, will add to his feast of reason, if not to his flow of soul.

The descent of the cliffs, at this point, is altogether too steep for safety or ease. To get to the beach, therefore, the rambler must turn off from the poorly-defined road through a deep cut just before reaching the light-house. The beach should be visited for the sake of its pebbles, which are the best shaped for paper weights to be found on the island, for the most impressive view he can find of the bold, rugged heights that there confront him, to best hear the grating of each receding surge, and to feel the majesty of the in-rolling billows.

If the evening be not too chilly, one should linger near the light-house until the sunset is over and the beacon in the picturesque tower is lit for the night.

The second visit to this point should be paid just after a southerly gale, and should be brief if there is still any wind, as it will be difficult getting about, and uncomfortable keeping still. But the magnificent massiveness and power of the waves, the exquisite beauty of their color and outlines, the passion of their white tossing crests, and the awful violence with which they break on the "cold grey stones," especially if beheld in a somewhat King-Canute-like proximity, and the wild aspect of a raging sea from the summit of the cliffs, are too rich a treat to be missed by any one possessing the least susceptibility to nature's grandeur.

THE NORTH LIGHT-HOUSE, CLAY HEAD, AND SALT POND.

There is little that is inspiring in the trip to the northern extremity of Block Island ; but whoever gets imbued with the generally languid and pensive spirit of this resort will find pleasure in the enterprise, aside from the satisfaction of having completely traversed the little ocean-girt domain which is his temporary home. The drive is somewhat longer than to the south cliffs—a mile further, perhaps ; the roads are so sandy most of the way as to make the ride more tedious, the shore

3

is low and desolate, and the light-house, a low, turreted frame building which has been moved shoreward from its old position out on the long reef, is almost as devoid of attractions as a weather beaten barn. Yet the ideal forlornness of the region will, for many, nevertheless have a charm.

Clay Head, the high bluff that bounds the wide eastern bay on the north, possesses some little attractions for the pedestrian, one of them being the glimpse of the distant castle-like light-house against the southern sky; and those who are equal to it will enjoy the stroll up the bathing beach, around the base of the prominence, and so on toward Sachem's pond, where he will meet those of his party who have driven. As there is but one wagon road going up from the harbor, one cannot lose his way driving; but in coming back he needs to be on his guard against the westward turn at the fork which is laid down on the map.

One cannot but be impressed with the loneliness of the sand hills along his route on this expedition, with the power of the wind which shapes them, and of the waves which in winter dash over them to rejoin the waters of the Great Salt pond; and he cannot but wonder, too, at the thriftiness of the tall bent on these grotesque and arid hummocks: a sort of vegetation, which, like the long, sprangly sea-weed rooted to the pebbles in the water's edge, forms a contrast with the luxuriant lawns and sensuous hot-house growths one elsewhere sees, forcibly illustrating the strange vitality of nature, and strongly suggestive of a sort of moral heroism.

The almost complete absence of trees, I think, is more keen-ly realized on this than on any other excursion about the island, the few stunted or twisted exceptions grouped about a private place of burial, here and there, only serving to more effectually prove the rule.

Off to the westward is the huge inland lake, which once connected with the ocean on both sides, and made two islands of what is now but one. It has an area of about a thousand acres, and its waters are still salt—a flume over on the western shore communicating with the sound. Numerous attempts have been made to raise oysters in its bed, but with compara-tively poor success; but there are some good perch to be caught there, and the pond has, within a year or two, been stocked with black bass. One of the original plans for making Block Island a harbor of refuge for the large coasting traffic was to cut a channel through from this vast reservoir; and a great quantity of soundings and calculations were made by an officer of the United States coast survey, to ascertain the prac-ticability of the scheme, which was finally abandoned.

Sachem's pond next to the largest body of water on the island, is about as prosaic as such a bit of scenery could be. And the beach of Cow Bay, as the indentation between Clay Head and the light-house is called, is interesting only to the coasters, who resort thither for loads of cobble stones to pave some distant city.

It was on the narrow strip of land, between the inland and outer seas, which one sees off towards the setting sun as he turns homeward, that the debris of the Palatine came ashore. Now and then an islander can be found who owns a trinket which once belonged to a passenger on that historic vessel. And it is still possible, though with great difficulty, to procure from some native a cup and saucer that were among the spoils of the wreck. Equally rare is the sailor who will admit that he ever saw the fiery phantom ship; though when his natural reserve is once thawed out, the Block Islander will tell you many an incident of the story which Whittier has so beautifully embodied in verse, and of the wrecks of the Warrior, and Metis, and others of those awful disasters once common on this coast, but now, thanks to the provision of a paternal government, fast becoming rare.

GOVERNMENT LIFE SAVING STATIONS.

Not far from the landing, next to a blacksmith's shop at a bend in the road, stands a broad-eaved cottage-like little edifice that soon attracts one's notice, and which he is told is one of the two life saving stations on the island, the other being over on the western shore. The building, with its furniture and management, is substantially the same as hundreds of others along the coast of the United States. The structure is 18 by 48 feet, and a story and-a-half high. The apartments within are provided with boats and apparatus, and fitted up for the occupation of the keeper and his crew, and the temporary shelter of as many as a hundred possible castaways. There are stores, household furniture and provisions on the lower floor, with cots and bedding aloft.

During the seven months of the year the establishment is closed, except in case of special emergency, although Captain Card, the keeper, can sometimes be persuaded to give the curious a look within. The regular service at the station is from the middle of November to the middle of April, during which time a crew of eight men are on duty, and a patrol is kept up along the coast in storms and thick weather. These men are vigorous, vigilant, bold and trustworthy, and are held strictly accountable for whatever property may be committed to their keeping in time of disaster.

Among the apparatus of the station is a life-boat twenty-seven feet long, with curved ends, flat bottom, shallow keel, air chambers at both extremities and along the sides just under the gunwales, and so ballasted as to right itself when overturned by a heavy sea. It requires a crew of seven to man it. There is also a small surf-boat, a mortar capable of throwing fifteen hundred feet of line, a mortar carriage, lines, hawsers, rockets for signals and the like.

THE BREAKWATER.

A long, straight pile of ragged granite, to whose black, wet base, at low tide, one sees clinging huge masses of yellow seaweed that sway with every ripple, is one of the first features of the island the visitor notices, protecting, as it does, the harbor

which receives him. Its principal advantage, at first, seems to
be the shelter it affords the pleasure boat of the summer visitor.
Then it dawns on one that the fishing industry of the island is
an important one, and is pursued at a time of year when landing a boat from an ordinary beach, beaten by an eastern sea
unbroken for thousands of miles, is a dangerous if not impossible undertaking. He learns, too, that until within a few
years the fishing boats had no other moorings than a little
forest of tall stakes, worked into the sandy bottom of the harbor, and looking like a magnificent growth of sedge; and that
passengers coming hither were brought ashore from large sailing craft in row boats. Finally, he remembers the immense
number of vessels engaged in the coasting trade, and which
always run for shelter in stress of weather; realizes how far
out of the way New London and Newport are, in such emergen-
cies, for vessels passing to the southward of the island, as most
of the coasters do; and so sees the propriety of the federal government stepping in, with its treasure, to make more safe the
life and property of a large class of its citizens.

The breakwater, at this writing, (April, 1877) is, as yet, incomplete. Its first stone was laid in the summer of 1870; it is
now twelve hundred feet long, having cost $205,000 thus far;
and its direction is north of north-easterly. Appropriations to
the amount of $60,000 are still unexpended, and contracts for
the continuation of the work have lately been let. It is pro-
posed to put in a bulkhead at the extremity of the already
constructed pier, to preserve a channel three hundred feet in

width, and then build an extension running due north. A range light, consisting of two beacons at the seaward and shore ends of the portions already finished, will ultimately be added.

THE CHURCHES.

The sectarian character of the old Rhode Islanders who colonized here was very naturally Baptist, and the two religious societies on the island are of that denomination. One, whose edifice is off toward the south-western part of the island, and whose pastor in 1876 was Elder George Wheeler, is too far away to possess much interest for the summer visitor. That located on the map is of close communion proclivities, and presided over by the Rev. S. T. Livermore, a gentleman of such originality, piety and force as to interest even the irreligious. It is well worth attending for the sake of hearing him. More than two centuries ago the original settlers of Block Island designated a certain plot of ground whose revenue should be devoted to the maintenance of religious worship, and the amount thus accruing, a trifle over a thousand dollars annually, is now divided between the two churches. To this is added the voluntary contributions of the members, and the donations of temporary residents: amateur concerts, dramatic readings, and other similar entertainments being given by summer boarders every year in their behalf. Services are also sometimes held in the parlors of one of the hotels, or at the restaurant down near the breakwater, Sundays, by either local or visiting clergymen.

LOCAL ANTIQUITIES.

Ancient as is this settlement, the place has few antiquities of interest to the visitor beyond the old cemetery, of which more anon. There are few traces of the Indians, except the names "Indian Head Neck," and "Sachem's Pond," and the old stone down near the south-west corner of the island on which the Indians are said to have lit their council fires. No pottery or implements of aborigines, unless it be now and then an arrow head, I believe are ever plowed up: indicating that the red men only made the island a transitory home. The relics of former wrecks I have already alluded to. No existing houses here that I know of possess any historic interest, the old fashioned church with high pulpit and box pews having not long since been demolished. Mr. Simon Ray Sands, an elderly and good natured islander, who can tell rather more of the history and topography of the place than any one else who has not made it a special study, has in his possession the original draft of the island, showing the apportionment of land to the first settlers, from two of whom he is himself descended. Mr. Sands' map and homely courtesy, are well worth seeking by the visitor.

AUNT BETSEY DODGE.

Another resident who is full of reminiscences, and who is more of a celebrity than Mr. Sands, is "Aunt Betsey" Dodge, whose humble dwelling, an old yellow house half way between the drug store and the Beach house, is sought by scores of visi-

tors every year, and who seems to be regarded as one of the
prominent institutions of the island.   Few people come to the
island without seeing, and none without hearing of this industrious old lady, who aside from "bringing up" a family of six
sons and a daughter, and like all the other native women doing
her own household work, has for forty years devoted herself to
the old fashioned hand loom.

In her seventy-sixth year, stimulated by accounts of "smart"
old ladies, she determined to show that Block Island could produce the equal of any of them; and her efforts that year re-
sulted in one thousand yards of carpeting, and four hundred of
flannel: an achievement of which she is justly proud, of which
she likes to tell, and which is enhanced by the fact that she did
her own housework meantime, and was absent from the island
on a three weeks' visit, the latter being an unusual circumstance
in the life of the Block Islander of her age and sex.

Through the persuasion of her sons, who are well-to-do fishermen or farmers and want to see her pass the remainder of
her life in ease and quiet enjoyment, she has finally abandoned
her labors at the loom.   Like Othello, her "occupation's gone"
and she misses the cumbrous old machine as one might a dear
lost friend.   Not satisfied to be idle, she now amuses herself by
knitting mittens and stockings, which are purchased season
after season by the callers who throng to see her.

She is a bright, wide-awake old lady and very original in
conversation; and as she thoroughly enjoys company, and always has a pleasant welcome for those who go to see her, she

is rarely alone. One kind friend last summer presented her with a gold finger ring, which, being the first she ever possessed, she prizes highly, and declares it shall be buried with her.

She has attained her eighty-first year, and in spite of her laborious life is still vigorous and has every prospect of a much greater age. Having a sister who has reached her ninety-seventh year, it is not improbable that "Aunt Betsey" may yet complete a century.

THE OLD CEMETERY.

So mildly interesting an enterprise as a visit to the old cemetery, whose whereabouts one can easily learn from the map, is not altogether wanting in pleasure to most visitors on the island. This graveyard is the principal one here, having been in use from the first settlement in 1661. There are perhaps a dozen family burying grounds, parceled off from corners of farms, here and there, but they are modern and without attractions. There are also a new cemetery, not yet used, and a burying ground for negroes, devoid of head stones and likewise of interest. During the Revolution, small pox raged here to such an extent that a hospital was erected near the south-west corner of the island, and the mounds which mark the last resting place of the victims are said to be still discernible. They are not worth seeing, however, nor are the graves of the Palatine's and other ships' dead, which have been buried over on the west shore, but without tombstones bearing inscriptions.

Even though one has but little antiquarian instinct, however, he can hardly fail to get some little gratification from a ramble in the old central cemetery, especially if he can prevail on his companion to search out the more interesting headstones, lie down on the grass to pull away the earth or scrape off the lichens, and read off the dim and imperfect but often curious epitaphs.

Unlike most graveyards, this is lacking in shrubbery, trees and lot boundaries; the grass grows long and tangled; the crumbling head stones are heaved out of place by the frost; and altogether the place has a most antiquated and lonely air. The symbolic ornamentation, the antique orthography, and the form of the lettering, are in many cases exceedingly rude and peculiar; and even more quaint are the sentiments sometimes to be found.

Few of the epitaphs are in verse; and yet these few are interesting for the beauty or odd mixture of the sentiment, the rudeness of the rhetoric, or the peculiar force of some word. Here is one, for instance, that for deep piety and ancient simplicity is fairly typical of the primitive New Englander:

> " I have a God who changest not,
>   Why should I be perplexed?
> My God who owns me in this world
>   Will own me in the next.
>
> My dearest friends who dwell above
>   I soon must go to see ;
> And all my friends in Christ below
>   Will soon come after me."

Nor can one fail to see the tenderness of true affection and the grace of Christian resignation in the following, incomplete as is the embodiment, and abrupt the change from the one to the other :

> " How fondly we loved her
>   No language can tell ;
> Grim death hath deprived us
>   And yet all is well."

A third runs thus, the glass referred to doubtless being that in which run the sands of life :

> " Stop, reader, spend a mournful tear
> Upon the dust that slumbers here ;
> And while you read the state of me,
> Think on the glass which runs for thee."

It is impossible to determine the age of the oldest grave in this cemetery, as some of the inscriptions are obliterated, some of the stones broken, and some gone altogether. The one last quoted bears date of 1765. Another quaint one is " In memory of Ackurs Tofh, who died June ye 2Jst, J739, in ye 54th year of his age." One finds plenty of dates of eighteen hundred and something. Soon he crosses the century line and strikes the seventeen-eighties, and sixties and forties ; and these latter soon set him at his mathematics and his English and American history. You find, after a while, the huge slab with the long tribute engraved thereon to Simon Ray, one of the original settlers, who died in 1737, in his 102d year, and you say to yourself, " Hundred and two from seventeen-thirty-seven leaves sixteen-thirty-five," and find yourself back in Charles the First's time, only fifteen years after the Pilgrims landed. I found several dates of 1730-odd, and one of 1708. Here's one that goes still further back:

"Here lyes intvrred the body of Mr. Iames Sands, Seniovr, AƆED 73 years. Departed this life March yᵉ 13, 1695."

This man was an original settler of the island, and was born two years after the Mayflower came to Plymouth rock, or two hundred and fifty-five years ago. The form of the letters in this epitaph is very quaint, and the engraver has gotten his " G" in "aged" hindside before. A peculiar shaping and combination of letters, which modern typographic art cannot easily reproduce, is to be found, too, in the following:

"Heare Lieth the body of Margaret GVTRY, aged 64 years, who departed this life April 3, 1687."

This is the oldest stone I have been able to find in the Block Island cemetery, and takes one back within a decade of two centuries. I have heard, however, of one bearing date of 1684, but never saw it. But one will find much to entertain him in his researches on this spot, even though he does not see all of the stones I have here mentioned.

TO BLOCK ISLAND AND BACK THE SAME DAY.

It has been my aim in the preceding pages to point out, to those visitors who come to Block Island for several days or weeks, the more prominent places of interest, and to offer a few

suggestions regarding the best way to reach and enjoy them.
I can hardly expect that every one else who visits them will see
them with my eyes : my only hope is to partly assist him in
becoming familiar with what is at first sight unattractive if not
forbidding, and to overcome the unpleasant impression he is
likely to receive from his first glimpses.

Much less do I expect to have helped the excursionists who
go over to the island with the intention of returning the same
day. Yet to them, a single word : So short will be your stay,
that you cannot see much of the island except right about the
harbor. You will hardly want to spend your time on a bath ;
and unless you secure a team immediately on arrival and make
haste, you cannot reach either Beacon Hill or the south light-
house, and get back before your boat leaves.

Nevertheless, a quiet lunch on the crest of the bluffs just
south of the breakwater, a ramble on the beach below, a
clamber to the top of the Ocean View hotel observatory, a
dinner at some of the hotels, a stroll inland to the springs or
some of the ponds on the way to the Highland house, or a little visit with friends who may be staying on the island, will
add much to the enjoyment of the visit. Every excursionist
should go ashore and look about him ; but if he does not, the
day's sail, the cool, salt air, the exhilaration of the sea, the
study of one's fellow passengers, the bustle and incidents of
the several landings, and the complete change of thought, will
amply repay the trip. The jaunt will afford a vast refreshment
to care-worn business men, over-worked artisans, exhausted and

heart-sick mothers, tired housekeepers, listless young folks, and eager children. Try it and see.

A FEW PRACTICAL HINTS.

For the benefit of those who come to the island for a protracted stay, I would offer these few closing hints:

Bring clothing fit for fall weather. It is quite cool most of the time on the island, and sometimes chilly. Block Island is a good place to wear out your last year's clothing, and especially for the children to knock about in. The best toys you can bring for the youngsters are books to press sea-weed in, and little wooden pails and iron spoons for digging in the sand.

Bear in mind that the moist sea air will shrink your woolens perceptibly, and calculate accordingly.

Unless you are too particular, bring a lot of paper collars and cuffs; the dampness will take the starch out of your linen.

Expect your scissors and other steel trinkets to rust somewhat.

Take an extra woolen shawl to spread on the beach or grass, or for a cushion or wrap when boating. It will prove a great convenience.

A private camp-stool will prove a handy thing at times, and unlike chip hats, can not be gotten on the island.

If you have a good pony and phaeton at home, do not live too far off, and can afford it, bring them along, by all means; you will hardly regret it.

Do not count on getting spirits on the island; bring your own brandy flask.

Arrange with some friend at home, if you can, to send you fresh fruit : it is scarce on the island.

If, in spite of advice elsewhere given, you determine to do much reading on the island—and if you are unwell for two or three days and are cooped up in doors, maybe you will get a chance—a previous understanding with the manager of some circulating library in Norwich or Providence will not come amiss. For fresh telegraphic news rely on the Norwich Morning Bulletin, which can be had at the boat three times a week.

Have your letters addressed to ." New Shoreham, R. I.," instead of Block Island, the former being the name of the post-office; and have the name of your hotel put in the lower left hand corner, or it will mislead some bungling postal official into sending it off to some of the cities after which several of the houses are named.

There is no telegraph line from the mainland to the island. A message to the Captain of the Block Island boat on Mondays, Wednesdays and Fridays, if received at Stonington before 10.30 A. M., or to the Captain of the Canonicus Tuesdays, Thursdays and Saturdays, at Newport by the same hour, would doubtless be delivered at any hotel designated.

As at other places, it is well to exercise caution about drinking the water of this locality too freely at first. The water at the springs, though, is perfectly pure and healthful.

It will be discreet to arrive at an understanding with your

host immediately upon coming to the island, relative to the cost of your daily trips to the beach, and the occasional use of a team for excursions hither and thither. Also to insist upon the regular attendance of the team for the beach every day, without specific instructions each time. At one or two of the houses this precaution will be necessary; but if acted upon in the right spirit, no difficulty need be anticipated.

Another desideratum at some of the houses is an understanding among the guests themselves to secure simultaneity in bathing, and proper care of the bath-houses which are owned severally by the hotel proprietors.

Lastly, when you come away, don't fail to bring your guidebook with you as a pleasant souvenir of your stay upon Block Island.

TIDE TABLE.

The following table will show bathers at Block Island the time of high tide for four months of 1877. It is unnecessary to add that the interval between high and low water is about six hours.

JUNE.	JULY.	AUGUST.	SEPTEMBER.
1.......11.24	1 ....11.27	1........12.07	1 ...... 1.33
2........12.09	2 ....12.07	2........12.58	2... .... 2.45
3........12.56	3........12.50	3........ 1.54	3......... 3.59
4........ 1.39	4........ 1.36	4... .... 3.00	4...... . 5.08
5 .... 2.29	5........ 2.30	5.... ... 4.12	5 .... 6.08
6........ 3.19	6.... ... 3.28	6........ 5.22	6........ 6.58
7........ 4.08	7... .... 4.30	7... ... 6.26	7 .... 7.43
8........ 5.02	8... .... 5.35	8... ... 7.19	8 .... 8.29
9... .... 5.56	9... .... 6.37	9........ 8.10	9..... . 9.12
10........ 6.49	10........ 7.31	10........ 8.56	10........ 9.56
11... .... 7.39	11........ 8.28	11... 9.40	11........10.18
12........ 8.40	12. ...... 9.19	12........10.00	12 ..... 10.40
13........ 9.32	13... .... 9.41	13........10.22	13........11.36
14........10.00	14 ....10.05	14 .. ....11.08	14. ......12.31
15... ....10.23	15........10.51	15 ......12.09	15........ 1.34
16... ... 11.19	16........11.39	16.... ...12.56	16........ 2.37
17....... 12.09	17........12.29	17........ 1.56	17....... 3.40
18..... .. 1.02	18........ 1.22	18.... .. 3.00	18........ 4.34
19........ 1.56	19........ 2.23	19 .... 4.04	19........ 5.23
20........ 2.51	20........ 3.23	20........ 5.04	20........ 6.06
21........ 3.48	21........ 4.22	21........ 5.56	21 .... 6.43
22........ 4.46	22........ 5.23	22.. ..... 6.40	22... .... 7.17
23........ 5.40	23... .... 6.17	23...... . 7.16	23........ 7.50
24 ...,... 6.33	24........ 7.03	24....... 7.52	24........ 8.27
25 .... 7.19	25........ 7.44	25........ 8.28	25....... 9.05
26........ 8.06	26....... 8.27	26....... 9.02	26 ...... 9.52
27 ...... 8.51	27........ 9.03	27.... ... 9.35	27... ...10.26
28 ...... 9.31	28 ..... 9.36	28........10.08	28 ....11.18
29....... 10.07	29........10.08	29........10.48	29 ....12.17
30 ....10.47	30...... .10.46	30........11.36	30........ 1.23
... .	31........11.24	31........12.30	... .

ADVERTISING APPENDIX.

STEAMER TO BLOCK ISLAND

—FROM—

Norwich, New London and Stonington,

AND RETURN.

———

THE NORWICH & NEW LONDON STEAMBOAT CO.

DURING THE SEASON OF **1877**,

Will run a Steamer from Norwich, New London and Stonington
to Block Island and back,

Mondays, Wednesdays and Fridays,

BEGINNING ABOUT **JULY 1st.**

The Boat will leave Osgood's wharf, in Norwich, at 8.30 A. M., New London at 9.30, (or on arrival of train from Hartford, Springfield, Willimantic and Norwich), and affording a stay of two or three hours.

FARES AT POPULAR PRICES.

PALMER SMITH, *Manager*, Norwich, Conn.

The Favorite Sea-Going Steamer

CANONICUS

WILL MAKE THE EXCURSION

From Providence to Block Island

—EVERY—

Tuesday, Thursday and Saturday,

DURING THE SEASON OF **1877, commencing Thursday, July 5th,** AS FOLLOWS:

Leave Fall River Iron Works Company's wharf, Providence, (east side), at 9 A. M.

RETURNING—Leave Block Island at 2.45 P. M.

Touching at Newport each way.

Fare, - - - - 75 Cents.

Excursion Ticket, to return same day, $1.00.

(iv.)

New London Northern Railroad.

Trains on this line connect with the Central Vermont Railroad; with Boston & Albany road at Palmer; with Hartford, Providence & Fishkill road at Willimantic, (to and from Hartford without change of cars); and with Norwich & Worcester road at Norwich; connections are also made at convenient hours, at New London with trains for New Haven, New York, Providence, Westerly, Stonington, &c.; and with Steamers for NEW YORK,

BLOCK ISLAND, WATCH HILL,

GREENPORT AND SAG HARBOR.

Ask for Tickets via New London Northern Railroad!

(v.)

NEW YORK & NEW ENGLAND R. R.

Norwich & Worcester Division.

(From Norwich, Conn., to Worcester, Mass).

Connects at New London with Steamboats of the Norwich and New York Transportation Company for New York ; and with Express Trains for Boston, Worcester, Nashua, Lowell, Fitchburg, Rochester and Portland.

Trains leave New London at 1.40 and 4 40 (Mondays excepted), Norwich at 2.25 and 5.20, 6.00, 11.45 A. M., and 4.45 P. M.

Trains leave Worcester at 6.45, 10.00 A. M., and 5.00 and 8.05 P. M.

P. ST. M. ANDREWS, Supt.

CROCKER HOUSE,

NEW LONDON, CONN.

By far the Largest and Finest Hotel in the City!

Although this house has been established but a few years, the excellence of its table, the neatness of its furniture, the modesty of its rates, and the courtesy of its management, have made it widely popular.

Travelers passing through the city should try its fare in preference to that of railway eating houses.

D. KELLOGG, Proprietor.

HIGHLAND HOUSE,

BLOCK ISLAND, (NEW SHOREHAM), R. I.

Entirely new in construction and appointments, and ready for guests the first of June. Finely located, and commands a wide view of the island and ocean beyond. Terms, moderate. Address

D. A. MITCHELL, Proprietor.

SEA-SIDE HOUSE,

BLOCK ISLAND, (NEW SHOREHAM), R. I.

Nearest Hotel on the island to the bathing beach: Accommodates limited number of guests comfortably: The best of plain fare, and the conveniences of private boarding-house. Terms, moderate.

Address   FRANK WILLIS, Proprietor.

(vii.)

OCEAN VIEW HOTEL,

BLOCK ISLAND, (NEW SHOREHAM), R. I.

FINELY LOCATED,   WELL APPOINTED,
SPACIOUS,   POPULAR.

NEAREST HOTEL TO THE LANDING.

☞ OPEN ONLY THREE SEASONS ☜

AND DURING THAT TIME HAS

QUADRUPLED ITS ACCOMMODATIONS

TO MEET

INCREASING BUSINESS.

CHOICE FARE,
MAGNIFICENT OUTLOOK,
PROMPT ATTENDANCE,
SELECT PATRONAGE.

This Hotel has a bathing beach and bath-houses of its own, scarcely
a hundred yards distant.

Terms, from $12.50 to $17.50 a week, or $3.00 a day.

SPECIAL RATES TO LARGE PARTIES.

NICHOLAS BALL, Proprietor.

(viii.)

PROVIDENCE HOUSE,

BLOCK ISLAND, (NEW SHOREHAM), R. I.

NEAREST HOTEL ON THE ISLAND TO THE OCEAN.

SITUATED ON A HIGH BLUFF
DIRECTLY OVERLOOKING THE WATER.

OPENED FOR THE SEASON OF 1876,

AND PROVIDED WITH APPOINTMENTS

OF A

MODERN SUMMER HOTEL.

ONLY A FEW STEPS FROM POST-OFFICE, AND NEXT DOOR
BUT ONE TO THE ISLAND DRUG STORE
AND LOCAL PHYSICIAN.

POPULAR, BECAUSE PLEASANT.

Terms, $9.00 to $14.00 per Week.

A. D. MITCHELL, Proprietor.

(ix.)

SPRING HOUSE

BLOCK ISLAND, (NEW SHOREHAM), R. I.

THE BEST KNOWN AND LONGEST ESTABLISHED HOTEL
ON THE ISLAND.

SITUATED ON A COMMANDING RISE OF GROUND, WITH
CHARMING SURROUNDINGS AND A SPLENDID
VIEW OF THE OCEAN;
SPRINGS OF MINERAL WATER HIGHLY COM-
MENDED FOR THEIR PROPERTIES CLOSE AT HAND, AND
FREE TO ALL GUESTS.

Extensive additions have been made to this Pioneer Hotel of Block
Island, within the past few months, vastly enlarging its capacity and increasing its attractiveness.   It will now accommodate a hundred and twenty-five
guests.   The dining room is lighted on three sides, the parlor is large, the
entrance (from north and east) wide and airy, and lodging rooms of good
size, and desirable.

TERMS, MODERATE;

The charges for apartments in the new portion of the house, however, being
greater than in the old.

Address B. B. MITCHELL, Jr., Proprietor.
(x.)

ADRIAN HOUSE,

BLOCK ISLAND, (NEW SHOREHAM), R. I.

———

This Hotel is situated on an elevation two hundred yards from the landing, scarcely ten minutes' walk ; but a step from the post-office ; and only a short walk from the bathing beach. It overlooks the bay and government breakwater, and commands an extensive view, reaching even as far as the cliffs of Newport on a clear day.

IT IS SURROUNDED BY A DELIGHTFUL LAWN, CONTAINS LARGE, COMFORTABLE ROOMS, AND ITS TABLE WILL BE SUPPLIED WITH THE BEST THE MARKET AFFORDS. DINNERS WILL BE PROVIDED ESPECIALLY FOR EXCURSIONISTS, ON ARRIVAL OF BOATS.

USE OF BATHING-HOUSES FURNISHED FREE TO GUESTS. CONVEYANCE TO THE BEACH OR BLUFFS, OR OTHER POINTS ON THE ISLAND, ON REASONABLE TERMS.

Board, From $7 to $10 per week, or $1.50 per day.

EXCURSION DINNERS, FIFTY CENTS.

For further information, address   CHARLES W. WILLIS, Proprietor.

(xi.)

BLOCK ISLAND, (NEW SHOREHAM), R. I.

———

This house, first opened for the season of 1876, was built in substantial and elegant style, with large, commodious sleeping apartments, large and airy dining hall, and all the appointments necessary for the comfort and convenience of summer guests. Will accommodate seventy-five people easily.

The proprietor promises as good accommodations, for the price charged, as can be found in the country—a table supplied with all the market affords, in its season, and other facilities offered by summer hotels.

TERMS,

$2.00 per day; or $10.00 to $15.00 per week.

HALSEY C. LITTLEFIELD, Proprietor.

THE HANDSOME NEW

SAIL BOAT JUANITA

Is owned by Mr. H. C. LITTLEFIELD, and can be secured for EXCURSIONS at the office of the above named Hotel.

(xii.)

WOONSOCKET HOUSE,

BLOCK ISLAND, (NEW SHOREHAM), R. I.

NEAREST HOUSE BUT ONE TO THE BATHING BEACH :
USE OF BATHING-HOUSES FREE TO GUESTS :
TEAMS FURNISHED for EXCURSIONS AT MODERATE RATES :
COMFORTABLE ROOMS : OBLIGING SERVANTS :
EXCELLENT DOMESTIC FARE : EARLY BREAKFASTS GIVEN
TO PARTIES GOING OUT FISHING :
ACCOMMODATES FORTY REGULAR BOARDERS :
DINNERS PROVIDED FOR DAY EXCURSIONISTS.
TERMS, UNUSUALLY LOW AND SATISFACTORY.

A. D. ROSE, Proprietor.

BEACH HOUSE,

BLOCK ISLAND, (NEW SHOREHAM), R. I.

Small, but admirably located on an eminence overlooking
the bay : Long a favorite private boarding-house
before the island came into general notice :
Good fare and attendance.

Terms, $1.50 per day; $7 to $9 per week.

M. M. DAY, Proprietor.

(xiii.)

(xiv.)

www.ingramcontent.com/pod-product-compliance
Lightning Source LLC
Chambersburg PA
CBHW021522090426